## Praise for *Pink Elephant*

Camacho's lovely and serrated debut collection reminds us why poetry as testimony is so necessary. Camacho does not romanticize victimhood; she simply means to show us how unchecked violence reproduces itself.

— Barbara Jane Reyes, The Poetry Foundation

*Pink Elephant* is the white elephant in the room blushing into visibility, and Rachel Camacho is a poet of unparalleled, unflinching honesty. With the tenacity of a survivor's "love-sharp teeth," Camacho confronts the trauma of girlhood/womanhood—"the malicious thunder of it"—and gives the "inaudible song of happiness" a palpable, perceptible shape. This book is startling testimony, and it will bruise the touch of all those who dare to turn its relentless pages.

— Rigoberto González, *To the Boy Who Was Night*

I literally woke up in the middle of the night thinking about these poems. They are compellingly beautiful with a perfectly-toned sadness. If these poems don't move you, you're dead inside.

— Bucky Sinister

# PINK ELEPHANT

# PINK ELEPHANT

poems by

Rachel Camacho

Button Publishing Inc.
Minneapolis
2026

PINK ELEPHANT
POETRY
AUTHOR: Rachel Camacho
COVER DESIGN: Amy Law

Published by Button Poetry
Minneapolis, MN 55418 | http://www.buttonpoetry.com

Manufactured in the United States of America
PRINT ISBN: 978-1-63834-138-3
EBOOK ISBN: 978-1-63834-142-0

First printing

*for my brother, who lived*

*for my father, who learned*

# CONTENTS

**PART III**



**PART IV**

**AFTERWORD**

# PINK ELEPHANT

# I.

# I FORGET WHO I SAID IT TO, BUT I REMEMBER HOW, AFTERWARDS, THEY LOOKED AT ME AS THOUGH I HAD DRIVEN A STEAK KNIFE THROUGH THEIR MOTHER'S HAND

*I love my brother. He had the exact same childhood as I did.*
*But he doesn't get credit for it. He isn't the writer. I am*
*the star of the violence. I expose. My Peter, when he marries,*
*I will be so sad. No girl in the world deserves him but me.*

## THE FIRST TIME

was after we realized God was
too busy for kids like us.
So we filled a shopping bag full of toys,
spoons and a jar of peanut butter

climbed the wall behind our apartment complex
and walked along the train tracks,
where we had sacrificed handfuls of pennies
and misbehaved dolls.

I was six years old, wearing a nightgown
and flip-flops, my brother, shirtless
in swim trunks
wearing no shoes at all.

It's funny to me now, picturing
two children running away
as unprepared as a fed up housewife—
where did we imagine we could go?
What new home would drop from the sky for us?
Which saint would dare bust from its plaster
shell to scoop us from our ugly lives?

Remember the awful moment you
figured out that what is yours is yours—
the maggots in the kitchen sink,
mother passed out on the porch,
how it felt after the third abortion,
that unrelenting itch in your heart?

It's why you are here now,
carrying a bag full of things
that will not help you, why houses
fill with those less deserving,

why saints hold their hands out
to everyone but you.

## HONEY

At the playground
we'd change our names for fun.
Jailed sand flies in our hands
until they'd sting to freedom.

Dirty-hair-smells-like-dog girl, Ruth,
became "Vanessa," who rode a limousine to school,
had a pet horse and an alligator, too.
One Monday, she showed up
with seven teeth knocked out,

*I fell down the stairs!*

(*Poor thing*) We gathered around her,
a jealous swarm of stupids, *Oooooing*
as she dragged her proud little tongue
across her red-raw gums.

*Just think of all the money she'll get from the tooth fairy!*
we squealed, as Vanessa stood in the sandbox,
a blinking new queen, while her daddy
sped to work in his old Toyota
tweezing the stinger from his hands.

## DOGGIE BAG ETIQUETTE ( STEPMOTHER 101)

On weekends, we'd crouch at the bottom of the door, listening to her
with our father. If they were fucking, it meant making breakfast

for ourselves, a twenty slipped under the door that night for pizza. If they
were laughing, waving the pot smoke out of their room through the window—

spaghetti for everyone. But if there was screaming, the crash of a body,
then silence—the phones were ripped out of the walls and we became

his children again. And the three of us would take off, my brother
and I on our best behavior in the backseat as he drove, paying good

attention as he read to us from the menu of a nice restaurant, the kind
where you leave money on the table
    if you were treated well.

## TOMBOY

The last time father took us to the beach,
I smuggled a mermaid into the car, kept her hidden
beneath a pile of blankets and wet towels.

After dinner, I snuck into the garage,
dragged her into my room by her slippery wrists.
She lived inside my closet for weeks,
smacking her rotting tail against the door,
its scales spilling to the floor like green coins.

I begged her to teach me the love in women,
to help me seem less unnatural.
But her words rippled in her throat—
a wild ocean language I could not comprehend,

*Give me something*, I warned, *or I'll dry you out!*
She began to writhe beneath my voice
as I spit words that slurred her flesh.

It was my own wild language, passed down
to me by my father: words, sounds, rages,
the darkest blue shades of misogyny
no child's mouth should ever dare commit.

I had given her everything. All that I'd inherited.
Allowed her into my home. Fed her, bathed her,
gave her somewhere to sleep. But she was full
of woman's ungratefulness and would not be seduced,
denying me the answers I knew she hid beneath her scales.
I stood over her, disgusted. Smashed a mirror against her breasts
then sucked the final splinters of moisture from her lips.

I did not sleep, just listened to her mouth wrench
and coil as her gasps surrendered into the little catches of air
she could find between tongue and teeth.

The next morning, I packed her throat full of sand.
Stuffed her gills with mud and broken seashells.
She lacked all strength to squirm and simply
looked to me in horror
watching me return to the only child I knew to be—

I was mythological and frightening.
I was half man,
I was half flawless.

## HOW FURY FINDS ITSELF

We found her crouched between two trash bins,
raw-bellied and thin, her white coat matted
with the blood of negligence. It was clear
she'd been attacked by better dogs,
by men who harm soft things to feel like men.

We tied a jump rope around her neck
and pulled her home, fed her stacks of bologna
and cat food stolen from our neighbor's porch.
My brother and I knew we belonged to her,
the way a heart knows it belongs to its ache.

We loved how well she hated our father,
how it only took her three days to learn what he was.
She'd bark at the sliding glass door,
stand on her hind legs, pawing at the screen
as he chased us shrieking down the hall,
kicking our bodies until our throats went sore.
After a week, she disappeared.
Crawled through a hole in the patio fence.
*Just like a mother,* father said.

It took seven years for him to admit what he had done.
That New Year's Eve, he staggered into the living room
and explained how it happened: how she fought so hard,
it took him and three other men to strap her down.
We sat quietly, watching each slurred crime spill
from his drink and flood our mouths.

That night, I learned vengeance can mean
one less knife at the dinner table;
an infuriated child tucked beneath
her father's bed, waiting.
Waiting.

# THE DOLL

After it happened, after the smack to the mouth
and the car ride home, after my braids were
chopped off and thrown in the trash,
after solitary confinement in a closet,
I pressed my ear against the wall, listening
to my father tell what happened over the phone,
his tongue sharper with each *yes* or *no*, or
*she doesn't know who he was.* His frustration
turned on me, the way fault can only be found
in the one whose name fits most in the mouth.

Crouched atop my father's work boots,
I decided to name the stranger. Not the man,
but his hand. Not each slender finger, just
the one. The one. When the light of the hallway
burned my eyes, and I was thrown into the bathroom
where he held my knees apart as she scrubbed scrubbed
scrubbed until I urinated to relieve the sting,
I caught my brother watching in the doorway,
and all my humiliation clawed its way to the surface
and I looked at him and said, *I hope you die.*
*I hope you die in hell with Satan.*

He stood motionless, as tough and
untouched as a boy could be in that house,
until my father said *Go* and he turned and went
to our room, climbed to the top bunk, safe
as a vulture. That weekend, we all had to stay
inside. No more parks. No more house keys
lost to cartwheels. So our cousins came to
visit. Little Jennifer, everyone's favorite,
equipped with a brand new doll, *Becky,*
hand-stitched by her mama, so there was no
way to duplicate such love, no store to snatch it from.

When all the children ran into the dining
room for lunch, I stayed behind, closing
myself in the bedroom. And I took that
doll, and I called her *whore. Bitch. Orphan.*
Then I twisted her up in my hands, mangled
her cloth body until I knew she felt it.
And then I shoved her down my pants,
rubbing her against the worst part of me
I could think of as I spoke to her between
my teeth, *Hello, pretty girl. You have*
*such beautiful long hair.*
*My name is Thomas.*
*What is yours?*

## WEATHER'S HERE, WISH YOU WERE BEAUTIFUL

There was the summer you ignored me so hard
it gave me bad posture. By fall, the chiropractor
prescribed a back brace and a name tag to wear
around the house.

Every Christmas Eve, instead of throwing me
a birthday party, you'd soak me in the bathtub,
fully-clothed, and hang mistletoe above all the light sockets.

I was never included in family portraits—
you said I had a face only a mother could leave.
I remember standing in your hallway every other weekend,
gazing at you and my stepbrother, wearing the framed smiles
I knew I would never inherit.

I became your biggest fan, chasing your car home
from the grocery store, standing outside your bedroom
for an autograph or a handshake, explaining,
*Ma, I've seen every one of your home movies!*
"Weekend Trip to the Zoo," "Mother/Son Picnic in Yosemite"
*and know every one of your mood swings by heart.*

When you'd drop me off at home, I'd brag to dad
and his girlfriend about my brush with fame. They'd smile
and nod, then shake the wild imagination right out of me.

Pretty soon the weekend visits faded into a nineteen-year
carnival line where I waited for you until the sights and sounds
of families and laughter made my stomach plunge.

That's the year I lost my appetite then found it
in men disguised as getaway cars. Sometimes a tingling sensation
sweeps across my face like an amputee's phantom itch,
and I realize how much I miss the back of your hand.

I know, I never apologized for steering you
into that marital car crash, but how was I to know
they'd pry your legs apart, drag me from the wreckage,
my first cries shattering that rear view mirror of a heart?

You could have told them. You could've explained—
I was just some filthy hitchhiker you never meant to pick up.
A greedy little fetus. An accident waiting to happen.

## A LIFE, IN SUBTITLES

In the beginning, all the joy is the joy you have and there is no one
foolish enough to try and take it from you.

This is your toy. Your birthday cake. Your mother. Your brand new
dog, your money, your sister, your private place—don't let anyone
touch you there.

Next comes: *it's broken, we ate it all up, she went to the grocery store*
*and she's not coming back, it died, you owe me, don't touch me,*
*please please let me touch you.*

In the car, while our father is pumping gas, we hear him arguing with
another driver. The man calls our father a *wetback.*

We play with the new word, let it build a second row of teeth
in our mouths. My brother and I are watching through the back

window. Our father glances over at us, knowing what has to be done.
The man turns his back, heading towards his car. My father unlocks

the trunk; violence acknowledging its audience. He strikes the man
in the back of the head. He collapses, immediately curls into a ball

on the pavement, neither man makes a sound as the body submits
to each determined swing swing swing swing

This is your father. This is a crow bar. This is a man in blood. This is his
quiet wife holding their baby. This is what happens.

*Read me a bedtime story. There are teeth in the parking lot. Get in the car*
*and go. She knew better than to try and help. There isn't a god*
*to stop me.*

# EASTER, 1981

1.

We found our Easter baskets hidden on the windowsill
and of course, had to count. We laid everything out
on the coffee table, examined our chocolate bunnies
in their blue sugar bow ties, counted each red jelly bean
to see which one of us father loved most.

My brother held up a large chocolate egg,
turning it in the light like a jeweler. I panicked,
scoured through the plastic grass, accused him
of hiding it, then shook out the basket one last time
until all that was left was inescapable surrender.
One missing piece of candy, sixteen daggers to the heart.

But what child could understand
what happened next? My father ordering
us to search our baskets again. The woman
I would never consider a woman nearly killed
for her assumed thievery; a rib cracked
against the door frame, wrists broken
for the face she tried to protect.

My brother licked the sugar from his fingertips
as I, the unknowing accuser, sat on the porch
watching the neighborhood children bounce past
our door in their clean clothes, holding
their parents' good hands, knowing how it feels
to be loved the most.

2.

We knew it couldn't be any other car but hers.
The malicious thunder of it, rolling up the street.
A biblical outlaw. A fiend unleashed.
Our mother dropped by to spy on us, didn't realize
it was Easter. She kept the car running and
swaggered down the sidewalk, stopping
in front of us, legs spread, a hand on each hip.

*Is that the bitch screaming in there?* She asked.
We nodded our heads. *He hits her too, huh?*
And I saw that she was pleased. Finally,
I had something. Something she could love me for.
*He does it all the time,* I said,
*You should have been here for her birthday.*

## THE DAY AFTER THE FIRST TIME WE RAN AWAY FROM HOME

My brother came into the bedroom
and told me he'd found our neighbor's turtle
on our patio, and he told me he lured it
to the back door with some lettuce,
and it ate out of his hand until the lettuce was gone,
and my brother didn't know what to do next,
so the turtle started to move on,
and this angered my brother, so he kicked it,
and it skidded across the pavement on its back
and it cracked against the garage door
and my brother felt bad but by then
there was no going back, so he sprayed
the turtle's head with Raid
and wrapped it up in a bath towel
and threw it into the garbage bin behind
the parking lot, and then he threw
more garbage on top of that, and then
he climbed into the bin and stomped the trash
down, and then he came back inside
and watched some television.

# PINK ELEPHANT

Two uneven braids crawl down
her spine, cheeks bright as a slap.
She is standing in the field behind
the house. The field he takes her to
when she's been bad.

She is careful where she steps;
the blind pit bull next door is let loose here
every day. To shit all over. She squats
in the tall grass, closes her eyes and slips

two fingers inside herself. Here it is Christmas.
She is a boy. Her bed doesn't smell like pee.
Here he was born without hands. Fireworks
pop secret messages in the air.

That night, a big silver dog will be waiting
on the porch. Who knows where it came from.
He looks like a wolf. His eyes blood dark.
They see everything. And one day he will drop
his shining fangs into her father's thigh, just before
his filthy boot clips her tail bone.

In a month, she will come home from school
to find the dog tearing at the man's throat
like a lamb chop. The girl will tuck in
her fat lip and smile.

He will show off for her. Chew each finger
down to its knuckle and place the leftovers
in her lap, palm-side up.

It will take nine years for the dog to learn to
walk on his hind legs perfectly. By then,
the girl will have become a woman
who has learned to wear dresses
and uncomfortable shoes.

They will hold hands and stroll through
the city. They will laugh and bite and
kiss like motherfuckers. Because he is still
a dog, he will continue to piss on fire hydrants.

This is something she will learn to tolerate.
Just as he will grow to ignore how, once a year,
she sneaks off into the field and gives birth
to a fingerless girl she buries
without giving a name.

# II.

## 814

It was the one place we were forbidden to ride our bikes:
the alley behind the liquor store, where our cousin had his own
bike stolen from him at knife point, forced to walk the carpet
of shattered glass, tied-off condoms and shot gun shells.
Graffiti sprayed over every garage door, the alley was a ghetto urinal,
filled with the territorial pissings of misspelled death threats
made by junior high dropouts.

Two of our uncles were in rival gangs. Vinnie claimed F-Troop,
Phillip repped Delhi. The stories they'd tell about the alleyway
dug through our hearts like dirtied miners, holding excavated chunks
in their ravaged hands. Jimmy Turnball, on angel dust, maimed a dog
with his bare foot. Jose Alvarez's body was found naked,
by his own mother, with someone's penis sewn into his mouth.

To get to the liquor store without cutting through the alley
meant riding around the entire 800 block with our backs
to the notoriously unhinged traffic of unlicensed immigrants
tearing through Bristol street.

It was summertime. I was ten, my brother, eight—
grown-ups in the latchkey underground. The milk money
left on the table was enough for four candy bars, two packs
of gum and a soda. We swore not to tell on each other
then sped down the alley, working our bikes through
a makeshift shrine to *vato locos*, dodging a balding pit bull
yanked back by its chain. We had almost reached
the end when a familiar smell hit the brakes.

I saw it first, tucked between a beat up car and garbage cans.
The definite hand, covered in ants. Blood snaked down
the driveway, work shirt nearly blown off, the thick buzz
of corpse flies working the holes. We stood over this man,
grateful we couldn't see his face. His namelessness
the only protection we had.

It wasn't a sadness I had known before—the weight
of this discovery drilling through my body, the immediacy
of death sprawled at my feet. We turned our bikes around
and went home, suddenly luckier to be alive, to feel
the afternoon sun biting through our shoulders,
to hear the siren of birds screeching in unison.

## THE SECOND TIME

we filled a suitcase with clothes,
emptied the coffee can of quarters
into a pillowcase and waited.

We timed our escape
around his snoring,
opening the front door
an inch for each noisy exhale.

My brother refused to
come with us, a betrayal
I would cling to for twenty-three years.

My father had locked the phones
in the trunk of his car.
The nearest pay phone
was across the street
in MacArthur park.

I called for the cab, my voice
bound by so much fear I had to
repeat our address six times.

My stepmother's nose was broken,
a collar of blood wrapped around
her nightgown, her scalp bleeding
where patches of hair had been.

She sat on the curb, holding a
tangled fistful of it in her hands.
It was absurd to watch her combing
through it, as if anything
could be salvaged.

Back in the apartment, she had crawled
on her knees, feeling around
for clumps of hair in the dark.

And I hated her for that. For being
nothing more than a woman,
hated her for the pity
I could not feel.

Forty-five minutes later, I was
sitting in the backseat of the cab
watching my father rage
towards us,
my stepmother frantically
rolling up her window
yelling at the driver *GO!*

Glass sprayed across our laps.
The driver began to scream,
my stepmother kept screaming,
and I could do nothing
but sit quietly amazed

as my father reached in
and pulled her out through
the broken window,
dragging the soft flesh
of her thighs over
an angry tooth of glass.

The cab sped off with our
suitcase still in the trunk.
I stood at the curb, holding
a bleeding sack of coins, waiting
for silence to overcome
the night.

The sprinklers came on
in the courtyard
as I made my way up the sidewalk,
following a trail of blood back
all the way home.

## FOR DU'A KHALIL

The morning I caught my brother behind the couch,
my pet hamster in his hands, holding her
steady as a bowl of blood, a new heat
moved through me, tightened itself
around my throat like a leash.

I smacked his face and bit his shoulder.
He dropped the hamster to the floor. An Easter present
from my father. *Mine.* I grabbed her
and held her up to his face,
squeezed until she went limp beneath the crush.

My brother couldn't say a word. I placed the dead thing
in his small hands and strolled down the hallway,
whistling like a prison guard. That night, I cried for hours
while all the house slept, blamed my brother
for the wilted spine of my beloved pet,
prayed for justice, begged the gods
to snatch him from his bed,
toss him to the snapping dogs
roaming the field behind our house.

Yesterday, I mourned a girl
discovered in the wrong boy's hands. A girl
whose uncles dragged her from her home, stripped
her down to narrow hips and undeveloped breasts,
slammed concrete blocks against her head,
her chest kicked in by a proud circle of men.

And their god swooned as blood flew from her
body like a swarm knocked loose from its home,
as teeth spilled from her mouth like fresh ripped pearls.

When they buried her beside a dog on the side of the road,
a small boy in the crowd watched quietly,
wanting to learn the softness of a woman

as my brother, sleeping 8,000 miles away,
sat up in bed with the dirt of my name in his mouth,
both of his hands hot and twitching.

## BEHIND OUR APARTM ENT COMPLEX, WHERE THE SKATE RINK USED TO BE

I was practicing cartwheels off the coffee table.
On the hundredth spin, my foot came down
on the lamp and it burst into pieces.
Peter, home sick from school,
came running out of his room
screaming, *What did you do that for?*
looking up at the clock, wanting to curse at me,
but understanding the importance of the clean up.
All the urgency and danger. He kneeled beside me,
plucking ceramic fragments out of the rug
as each minute spun the clock's hands into fists.
I bandaged my foot, wrapped the lamp
in newspaper and buried it in the dumpster.
Through dinner, Peter and I
sat in silence, ate all of our vegetables first,
drank down the milk and denied the offer of dessert.
We cleared our plates, went to bed and waited.

Do you ever watch a scary movie you've already seen,
but still yell at the girl limping around the house,
warning her to get out, the killer's right behind her?
And as you scream for her to run across the street
to the neighbor's, you think maybe she'll hear
you this time, take your advice and the movie
will be changed forever?

It is what I imagine my brother thought about
when we were awakened later that night,
pulled out of our beds by our hair,
Peter crashing down
from the top bunk, the fever
still blaring from his ear infection
as we were dragged to the couch,
our father holding his bloody palm in our faces,
screaming so loud he was hoarse the next day.

Maybe it was because I was crying so hard
I couldn't catch my breath enough to speak,
and after the seventh or eighth slap to the face,
my brother got tired of waiting
for my botched confession, that he stood up
and walked out of the living room,
slammed open the back door
leading to the empty field,
then glared back at our father and said,
*I broke it, okay? Now c'mon. Let's get this shit over with.*

## HOW IT'S DONE

To forgive my father means to uncover
the value of my own life. To admire
what had the guts to be cruel, to lie down
with it at the smallest hint of kindness
and donate this body to house
the few sweet things
that could come from it.

## FOR PETER'S SAKE

The first time I was molested
was on a church playground. Calvary Chapel.
My parents married there. Proud, I told my father
what happened. He smacked me like a housefly,
swung me into the car by my hair.
Whenever I tell this story, I am careful to leave out
how my brother stuck his tongue at me
the whole ride home.

## THE BALANCE

There were days when no one got hurt.
Entire weekends where the three of us would sit
around the house watching impossible horror movies,
eating chips on the couch. Still scared, but for smaller reasons.
Some nights, my brother and I would run up the block, pressing
our thumbs into the glowing doorbells, running and laughing
as our father drove alongside the sidewalk in a retired police cruiser
turned getaway car. We'd go to bed still panting and sweating,
listening to each other breathe in the dark, neither one of us
daring to speak a word that might pull us from the dream.
To live at all, I have to remember these days, too,
place them on the highest shelf like glass figurines caught mid-dance.
They are so important, I can hardly bear to hold them.
What if, one day, I reach up, and they are gone?
What if I imagined them just to survive?
It is the same thing I do with my children.
I wake up in the middle of the night and run to their rooms,
feel beneath the bed sheets for their tired warmth,
press my mouth to their faces as if to inspire them
(even if they are not really there, even if they
are soft, impermanent ghosts ) to stay.

## ORPHAN

Sometimes I wonder what it must be like
to be in the same room as your mother.

To be able to look at a woman's body
and say, *I lived there.*

## CALIFORNIA, 1984

> *"You don't understand me. You are not expected to. You are not capable. I am beyond your experience. I am beyond good and evil . . . "*
>
> —The Night Stalker, before sentencing at his trial

The newspapers said he targeted yellow houses
so I hated our apartment building—
its peach stucco exterior, shunned.
Then it was written he preyed
upon the elderly, deeming
my nine-year old body useless.
Too many of his victims were Asian
so I cursed my Mexican grandparents.

That summer, I learned, finally,
what a pentagram looked like,
and what it meant—
an emblem of fear stitched
upon the hearts of a god-fearing
America who could not comprehend
how a soulless man could
climb into our homes
to rape our wives and slit our throats.

And I, defiant as a swatted bee,
propped my bedroom window
open with a book and said his name
in the dark, the way a lonesome pig
might summon the butcher:
*Richard. Richard.*

Each morning, I awoke, soaked
in the piss of envy
as a new victim's name
staggered through our city
like a bloodied lamb.
Then the photograph: his face
on the television screen,
so sharp and empty
it seemed drawn on.

When he was captured,
he smiled for the cameras
and stuck out his tongue.
All the women in the
neighborhood became less
important, all the guns
were emptied, then put away;
and the stranger's hands
that finally found my body that year
were softer than I had hoped,

as if he were doing it more out of
pity than want, a monster
suddenly aware of the harmless
child standing before him,
a child who had discovered
every way to say *Please*
without saying it.

## THE LAST TIME

I did it alone,
without leaving.

The welt on my face
still hot, I crept downstairs,
pried open the toolbox
and grabbed the hammer
with his initials burned deep
into the handle.

Upstairs, my brother slept
in his room, a glass box
of reptiles watching over him.

I turned the knob slowly,
stood over my father's body,
his chest heaving, then sinking,
when his tongue rattled, then stopped,

and the whites of his eyes
rolled over, and he stared
only at the weapon in my hand
and I looked at him and said,
*If you ever touch us again,*
*I will kill you.*

And then he saw me.

*Okay,* he said.
*Okay.*

## THE INAUDIBLE SONG OF HAPPINESS

You wake up to a phone ringing somewhere in the house.
By its ring, you can tell it is a real phone, with a rotary,
the kind used by secretaries in the 1950s.
There is a man lying next to you you have never seen before.
He smells like powdered hand soap.
He is missing the index finger of his left hand.

You wrap the bed sheet around your naked body
and look for the phone in the kitchen. You know it is not
going to be there as the volume of the phone's ring
starts to fade. You open the refrigerator: empty,
except for a gallon of bad milk
and the dog you killed in sixth grade.

The phone begins ringing louder, as if it thinks
you have forgotten it. The hallway to the bathroom
is covered with picture frames, each one displaying
the same small boy perched on a different man's knee.
You find the phone in the medicine cabinet.
It is a large blue rotary dialer, just as you knew it would be.

You wait one more ring to answer it. *Hello?*
But there is no one on the other end. You can hear
a room full of voices in the background,
spills of laughter and party horns. A woman
is telling everyone to please quiet down,
it is time for the birthday song.

You imagine the woman carrying a birthday cake,
stepping slowly into an unlit room, her face
illuminated by an unspecified number of candles.
The people start singing. A man's voice can be heard
above the others. Clearly, he is drunk
and thinks his singing is the best.

You listen for the name of the birthday man or woman,
it has become very important to you. You want to know
whose party you were not invited to. Which one
of your friends is secretly an asshole.

But the voices are too many and the name gets buried in them,
setting off nine small explosions of grief inside you.
As the song ends, everyone cheers the unknown wish
blown into that place where all lost things go.
The laughter subsides, becoming softer
the longer you listen to it.

You are naked, crouched beside the toilet
with a phone pressed hard against your ear,
trying to hear your name come up
in the inaudible song of happiness.

## LOST DOG POSTERS
## NAILED TO TELEPHONE POLES

First, he dropped his popsicle
into the sandbox, then cried out
at every mouthful of grain.

He ran over to his mama,
all orange sap and grit-chinned.
Without looking up from her magazine,
she threw a napkin toward him
and pointed back to the sandbox.

He stood beside her for a moment,
staring at her like an old photograph,
then ran back to the playground
with bits of napkin stuck to his cheek.

As he climbed the wrong way up the slide,
I thought of the dog I had in fifth-grade;
how I yanked his tail when no one was looking,
how he'd yelp *for no reason*
when I was playing with scissors.

# AFTER THE BLACKOUT

Last night Crazy walked into the house
like he owned the fucking place.

*Hey, Rachel, I'm Crazy*
*and I own this fucking place.*

I nodded, went to the kitchen
and poured him a glass of milk.

We sat around my dim living room,
squinting and chatting.

I felt like I'd known him for years.

# CARDINAL

1.
When I stole your lover, you cut your arms.
Moved to a different town. Got raped and pregnant.
Ran to Illinois. Tried coke for the first time.
Drank all night before the nurse slid you
the emptying pills. Left your body
when the baby did. Fished it from the water
and named it.

2.
According to my six-year old son,
humans come from eggs pushed from
the earth's warm soil. He claims when he
cracked into existence, he chirped for me
all night long, and each deep green feather
that covered his body was slicked back in blood.

3.
In the hospital, my head thrashed like a crazed bee
locked in a jar. My back arced as my bones stretched
around a blue-faced girl. As they snipped the cord
wrapped around her throat, my phone rang
for the first time in twenty-six months. You told me
you were having a baby, *For real this time*,
as a nurse slathered my daughter's foot in cold black ink.

4.
Some say if you touch a baby bird,
dousing it in human scent, its mother will reject it.
This is a myth. The truth is, there are three things
that could happen—

You can reunite the bird with its family, and it will
live and prosper and, as fate would have it, one day
shit on your car.

or

You can name it and leave it in a cage. Give it
a newspaper to read. Feed it birdseed. Teach it
to sit on your finger, to watch television.
When it dies, bury it in a shoe box.

or

It will train its feathers to become skin. Break off
its beak and learn the language you speak.
Force itself to sing like ordinary men.
Discover the practicality of forks and knives.

5.
You're a mother now. You whisper into the phone.
Your boyfriend comes home late and drunk all the time.
You want to get out. You want a better life for your baby.
You named him after your father. You didn't see a doctor
the first six months you were pregnant. The moment he was
born, you learned how to love him. You held him in your arms.
Fed him worms from your mouth. When the nurse came
to take him, you pecked a hole into her hand. *This one is mine,*
you said, *I am his mother. No one else can touch him.*

## POEM FOR THE MISSING POEMS ABOUT MY EX-HUSBAND

Perhaps they have dug a hole in the courtyard to soak
their feet in the mud. Maybe they are thumbing through
magazines at a dental office in Minnesota, waiting
to have their cramping wisdom teeth pulled. I am sure some
have filled their suitcases with old love letters and submachine guns,
while others have chosen to free themselves of possessions entirely,
opting to live in an abandoned church, devoting themselves
to the God of Songlessness. Several New Yorkers claim to have
spotted one limping down St. Mark's, muttering something about loss,
about working overtime to pay for abortions and school supplies,
while another (the first one I ever wrote, actually, the one
vowing to fold my kisses into paper airplanes) sits alone
on a park bench, watching rats fight over a beer can
on an empty playground.

## ON ORDERING PAY-PER-VIEW PORN AT 5 A.M.

A cold nail peeked its crippled head from between
the floorboards, and thinking of my baby's tender knees,
I wanted to take a hammer and smash it down,
but it was too late or too early,
so I was left alone in the living room to stare at it,
to imagine what it will do to me or someone I love.

The year after high school, when I slept on park benches,
I would repeat my favorite words to myself
and I would see them form in the dark,
soft lines of cursive light—
*home home home*
*feast feast feast*

I wanted you to rescue me then, although
I was not sure who you were. A different face,
smaller hands, a mouth that could love me.

Turning my back on the nail,
I opened a window.
I asked you a question.
I said what I want.
(The girls in school taught me that.
Chant what you want and it will come.)

When you didn't arrive, I wanted to hurt
those terrible girls who left me here, a fool in the dark.
I yearned for a hard and just cruelty. I wanted them
to learn what an endless solitude is capable of.

I turned on the television. I watched them moan
and scream, my body lifting three inches
from the couch, their agonized faces
the opposite of the words they were saying:
*yes yes yes*
*yes yes yes*
*yes yes yes*

## THE ONE THING I CANNOT FORGIVE

is not the New Year's Day you came home nine hours late.
It is not our children sitting quietly at the window,
examining the faces of neighborhood men. It is not
how I imagined you, somewhere in a field: your eyes
locked like bloody fists, your face full of dirt and murder.

It is not the time I woke to you masturbating as I lay
naked beside you. It isn't how unnecessary I became,
the soft roar in your throat, the back of your head
twisting the pillow, your open mouth—
screaming, but not screaming.

It is not the time I told you *regular* and you
brought home diet, how I suck in my stomach now
when you undress me, put on lipstick getting ready for bed.

It is not when I overheard you ruin nine years of my hard work,
squinting the truth about Santa into our child's hopeful eyes.
It isn't even the sound her heart made as it fell over
like so many termites in an old tree.

It is not because you weren't cradling roses in the waiting room,
how you didn't hold my hand during the cab ride home.
It isn't how I cannot forget the two little names I had chosen.

It isn't the way you confronted my father, as if you yourself
had lived it. It isn't the mouthful of blood you never swallowed,
or the bottle of pills you have. It is not that ungrateful attempt
to end a good and comfortable life.

The one thing I cannot forgive stands between us at every hug,
its hot palm across my mouth when kissed. The one thing
I cannot forgive has a name I can't pronounce. Its sound—
a ripped photograph. A kicked face. A faded map.

The one thing I cannot forgive squirms inside me,
a dirty maggot. It is sharp as a little bitch and fatter than
the butcher. Floats in my stomach, an angry sole survivor.

## SACKETT, REPRESENT

On trash day, the air rattles
with the scent of soiled diapers
and grey meat left too long on a kitchen counter.

I've learned when to turn my head
before the lukewarm filth of New York
can grab my face like a naughty Labrador
and rub my nose in it.

Women travel in twos down Sackett Street,
grinding their mouths into gossip, pushing
matching strollers with matching white babies—
gold-haired, blue-eyed tots who will inherit
thick Jamaican accents from their nannies.

Men sit outside the barbershop in lawn chairs
tuning radios with wire hanger antennas
just two blocks from where Al Capone
married his startled Irish darling.

I want my daughter to grow on these streets,
want this life to bend towards her borrowed green eyes.
I want these cobbled sidewalks to remind her to keep unsteady.

I want the boy who will break her heart
to first scratch her name into the meat of his Italian forearm.
I want her to sneak a beer out on a fire escape,
get fucked in a basement, curse God for the first time
on a rooftop over the Hudson.

# DRIFT

*for Laci*

I was never taught to swim properly.
Mother told me not to worry. She said,
*The ocean keeps damaged women afloat,*
*breaks us from concrete blocks and alibis.*
A smooth seal nudges my gleaming torso.
My tethered fetus was snagged on fish hooks,
they sank their teeth into his chest and stole
his blue and unborn heart. Mermaids bang their
tails against the boats of men in protest,
gulls swoop down to snip the last of my breasts.
I don't mind being pecked by fish, I've fed
my body to the hungry for years now.
When my salted bones come crashing to shore,
all that I ask is you give them my name.

# MOLT

It started when she no longer wanted him
to see her naked. Confused, he pounded
on the bathroom door for nearly an hour,
begging her to let him in. To give him
one more chance. Something he'd learned
from a movie. A desperation chorus—
*Oh, please! Just one more chance!*

His small fists tender, he finally gave up.
Pressed his back against the door
and listened to her splash around with her dolls.
The plastic mermaids. Their mock drownings.

As his whimpers flooded the house,
you put down your book and laughed,
said something smart about growing up,
something about boys pounding at her door.
The water was running. I couldn't quite hear you.
I was pouring old milk out, into the sink.

## WORCESTER, MA CHRISTMAS 2003

When I met your mother,
I was amazed at how small she was—
a round little stopwatch, and you,
a grandfather clock. I imagined your arrival
was less of a birth and more of an unfolding.

Your parents spoke with their mouths full,
but my children wanted to become grandchildren,
so they did not stare and they didn't ask questions
about the woman growing in the attic.
They sat still through your father's sermons,
forgot the words that once dropped like stones
from my tongue: *hypocrites, statue worship.*

When I broke the news to your mother,
I could hear each word crash
against her face like a frying pan.
She was quiet for too long.
Then she asked, *But did you*
*actually see him do it?*
And that was that.

As you crammed handfuls of dirty laundry
into a suitcase, all I could think about
was that first Christmas morning
at your parents' house, when my children
snuck to the top of the stairs
and tip-toed across the attic floor.
It was the one thing they couldn't
keep their mouths shut about.

They howled about her the entire
ride home: *She just stared straight ahead*
*like a souvenir! Her feet weren't*
*touching the ground! Her hair crawled*
*across the ceiling like a wounded dog*
*and her skin made a slow red sound.*

# IV.

## A TEAR FOR MURDER

Turns out the teardrop I want
tattooed below my left eye means *murder.*
Although I think of it often,
I have not yet earned the mark.

The disabled pigeon on Dean Street
staggers beneath the weight of
his new meaning: *Heart.* Your heart—
dirty—a spinning grey hunger.

That chandelier in the lobby: a clot
of all your finest bones. Your blood,
its wet revenge, has stitched itself
into a quilt we've vowed to share.

There is a man inside your rotting tooth
you haven't spoken to in years.
As we kissed, I grew the urge to rip him out,
swallow him down for good. Instead,
I placed a teacup in the cabinet of your mouth.
It is full, but I can't say of what.

## WHAT COMES NEXT

I.

I can't explain why I made him read the letter back to me,
required his voice recount each crime, demanding explanations
when we knew there were none. What I do know is this: I wanted him
to learn the bottomless dark, to follow the trail of words down into the hole—

*hair*    *slap*    *closet*    *please*

needed him to see how it was written, in the neatest penmanship,
so there could be no mistake, no doubt each admission was as hard
to write as it had been to live.

II.

It is the same dream. My brother and I inside a big house,
fifteen stories high. We are on the top floor, feeling around an unlit
hallway, trying to find a room to fall into, but every door is locked.
And it isn't until we've reached the bottom that a door finally opens.

When we get outside, we remember we have nowhere to run to,
so we have to turn around and go back inside.

III.

It was late; everyone was sleeping. I was on my way out when
a small hand risked everything and passed an envelope to me
through the closing door. My son's voice in the hallway said, *Here.*

As I read it, all the years came back to me:
the crow bar. The field. The man with the soft white hands. The boy in a jar.
The severed thumb. The girl on the floor, biting off her tongue—
a life staring back at me, baring its long and yellow teeth, asked,
*What will you do now?* While the voices in the letter asked *When?*

IV.

The moment you can look at a man and see he is no longer your husband,
when his face becomes a father's clockwork mask, turning itself
past recognition, his voice a coward's hands dripping mud from
the grave he's dug, what other choice do you have but to defy your history,
become the god riot of your own small and meaningful world?

V.

Two children are walking up the road. They've followed a bread trail
all the way here. I open the door. Their faces, dirty and waiting.
Their bad posture tells me they know what comes next.
The older one, the girl, when she speaks,
always has her eye on the knives,

but the boy just eats and eats, tells jokes all night long, laughing.
And as he sleeps, the girl sits up in bed beside him. She never sleeps.
She is certain this is a world that would do nothing to protect them,
certain she knows exactly how this ends.

## THE PACIFIER

soothed you and mocked my shape
as a fever rang through you
like an angry bell, my breasts
sharp with abandoned milk.

I tried to pluck the pacifier
from your mouth when your sleep
seemed deep enough,
but your arms would startle
into reaching, your jaw
clamped young and strong.

It had been years since a breast
hung above me, heavy and desperate
for my mouth. I imagined my mama,
lying on her side that first night,
teetered by so much milk
as I rolled her body down to my ankles
and came into this world.

Father told me how she would tease,
rubbing her nipple across my lip
until my head whipped toward it

how she'd pull back and laugh
as I wagged my empty mouth,
rooting for her tough, sweet skin.

Sometimes, it wasn't a nipple at all—
she'd graze my cheek with her knuckle
or a lousy finger,
haunting my dumb and helpless face.

That is how I learned the difference
between women and mothers.
That is when I knew
what I wanted to be.

# POEM FOR MY LOVER AS HE PLAYS GUITAR IN BED

We ride into the first day of the new year
on shipwrecked zoo animals stained in blood
on the mattress. The children, dressed as pink canaries,
sing for food outside our door. I kiss their ears
and feed them my thumb for breakfast.

Today, the woman in my head is drowning.
You remind me why I was born and her lungs
fill up with fish. You lick my wrists
and her eyes turn to old salt.

I want to give you what you are.
My belly dreams of becoming a fat hot cauldron,
breasts dripping, sweet milk hives
for ten mouths shaped like yours.
You ask, *What if I can't?* and my ribcage
creaks like a cellar door. It's January. Dead of winter.
It hasn't snowed once all goddamn year.

## FOR THE BEAN

How strange to see you
not as some flopping thing
fighting for air,
but as a wet red pill
breaking down in the water,
soft and boneless, hands so young
they were not quite hands.

It was no small event.
I plotted with men I do not believe in,
cursed a forgotten mother, slept
perfectly still and dreamt of a doll house
with rat traps for doors—
everything I could do to hold you in.

By morning, you had outgrown me,
untroubled yourself of my belly's sweet habit,
my aging heart, its lonely greed.

I returned to a home filled with dying things:
the lamp in the bedroom coughing up light,
flowers in the kitchen all turned to wood.

I watched myself in the bathroom mirror,
surveyed my childless body
as drops of water sang in the sink,
the old rusty faucet dripping, gently.

## WHERE I RETURN TO YOUR DEATH AS A POET

*for John, ten years late*

When my daughter rushes into the living room,
cheeks flushed from her wicked siblings who spring from closets

and unlit hallways, all the fear in the world blotched upon her
small round face, I pretend sometimes her body is being driven by you,

that you have discovered a temporary passage between heaven and bone,
and when I speak to her, I am really speaking to you,

and I know we haven't much time—
my daughter is young and must return to herself.

So I speak urgently, each word a tiny grain of sand, spilling.
It won't be long before she learns to repeat our conversations,

breaking the privacy, the awkward third lover. Already she
practices whispering into her hands, stands too long

in an empty room, stares through her father at the dinner table.
Each new year I feel the mud thickening beneath my feet.

One morning she will wake up too old to remember any of this,
delivering to us your second death. I am sure I will know it

the moment it happens. The first time she comes home a few hours late,
enters the house a woman I do not recognize.

## INVISIBLE LIFE

Jimmy went belly-up in the mason jar.
My daughter tapped on the glass with
a slightly interested fingernail. I nodded
my head. My son ran into the hallway
to investigate. *Jimmy's dead,* we said,
in our best deathly duet. My son shrugged
his shoulders. *Well, then, I guess he doesn't
get to have a name anymore.* He stood there
like a grade school principal, staring us down
in the hallway.

I felt like crying. *You mean, he doesn't get to be
Jimmy any more?* I asked, because I really didn't
know the answer. My son, plump with pity,
looked at the jar, then me, then his sister,
then back at the jar again. *I'm sorry, mom.
But that's just the way it goes. When you die,
you don't get to be anybody any more.*
And all of my unaccomplishments rapped
on my skull like a rock fist.

*Yes, sir,* I said, and I peeled the gold Jimmy suit
from the tiny skeleton and draped it across
the palm of my son's hand. *Good-bye, Jimmy,*
I cried, while my daughter rolled her eyes.
*No*, said my son, sternly, *not Jimmy. You have
to say, "Good-bye, deadness." Then say a prayer
for his invisible life.*

## NEW DOGS

It is the first good thing sweethearts try to do for each other—
replace everything their loved ones have lost.
A daddy here. A toy robot there. It is an impossible feat,
of course; some wandering dogs have since become
the bones for new dogs to chew.

There are friends who will
never slow down enough for the catching,
bad years that will forever hang in our hearts—
ghost-filled piñatas to swing a stick at.

It is why I have started small: replacing
the accordion you left with a friend, sold while you
held a hungry thumb out to passing cars, the shining
red bicycle lifted from a cut-down pole as you dreamt
of an empty plane seat in Louisiana.

I am not as good a listener as I am familiar with each story.
I know a father's inability to vanish, the seeds of revenge
we eat from his hands. I know the tarnished coin of a mother's love,
how it sleeps in a well, dark and unspent. I know, sometimes,
the most obvious things are what none of us would dare want back.

We live it out, imagining that, somewhere, there is a house
bursting through the soil, filled with hundreds of misplaced relics—
gifts for the grief-struck living, awaiting their turn.
The baby mice you were forced to flush. My brother
and your sisters sitting in a neat row on the mantel.
A cup of unspilled blood. The refrigerator, filled. Windows in every room,
overlooking a field of violets, facing the sun. The good gold sun.

## POEM AT TWELVE DAYS LATE

A dog of habit, a dog of agonizing
repetition, I cannot dissolve the terror
humming in my throat, the possibility
of you let loose in my body to develop
a new set of eyes and hands. An unfamiliar
child, roaming. Who have you come to
replace? Don't you understand, I fear
every introduction of joy? Each sweet
thing held in front of my heart's mouth?
Please, if you are there and mean no harm,
knock three times and I promise to need
you fervently. But if you intend to sway
the gods, to encourage a hawk to drop a
turtle shell upon my baby's dear skull,
if one of my boys gets carried away
by a stream of ants, my oldest daughter
stomped down to skinmilk by a flock
of stones, I will carry you as my mother
carried me—a defiant bride in a veil
of snakes.

## A SUNDAY CROSS-EXAMINATION OF MY FUTURE NEXT HUSBAND

In my father's house, beneath the floorboards,
where the wood is worn, lies a jar with a faded label.
Inside is a tiny daughter, pickled in rosewater,
her wrists held by twine. She sings a school of copper fish.
They move through the tangled pipes above her rotting head.
I hear them when I bleed. If you are to love me,
you must believe every word of this.
Every haunted girl you knew before me
has been a warning, and in the mouth of each girl:
a brick with my window's name on it.
I've watched a soul dance like smoke
from a mouth and burn through my hair.
I ate a plate of fingernails on my wedding day,
made vows as the bones of friends stirred the mud beneath my gown.
In four years, my husband's hands grew twice the size of his body.
I cut them down like men from a tree and hid them in a box.
They ghost the hallways of a sixth-floor apartment in Brooklyn.
My children are all five of my hearts, unleashed.
When I die, will you bring me flowers and a box of chocolates?
Will my going skin be your saddest song? Do you understand:
instead of becoming a woman you grow old with,
I want to be the god you run to?

## CENTRAL PARK, MOTHER'S DAY

My son comes to me, holding
thirteen severed tulip heads.
A present he's made just for me.

I knock the flowers from his hands,
grab him by the arm, move quickly
from the crime scene.

I explain: thc lake, the trees, flowers, birds—
do not belong to us.

I watch something bright and alive
go pale. His head lowers like those stems,
their broken necks.
Chin against his knees, he stares
into the grass. Does not speak again.

A mama forgets what her weapons can do.
Can't know which of her failures
will be what does it.
Tommy's turn with the belt, in fifteen years,
becomes Meaghan's throbbing black eye.

Christina's twisted arm
becomes suicide without a note.
Kevin's scolding at open house
becomes only girls when they're upside-down.

This morning, I found thirteen tulips
waiting nervous at the foot of my bed.
I gathered them in a blanket,
kissed each tiny face. Gave them names.
One is *The Crumpled Photograph I'll Find*
*of Myself in the Garbage.* Two, *The Dog*
*Smacked with a Tire Iron.*

Three, *The First Time He Says "Fuck You"*
*and Means It.* Four, *The Heavy Girl He Can't*
*Bring Himself to Love.* Five, *My Empty Wallet.*

Six, *Hardened Piss and Vomit on the Carpet,*
seven, *A Lock on the Bedroom Door,*
eight, *The Word "Faggot" Scratched*
*Across a Face in the Yearbook.*
Nine, *The Eighth Time He Says "Fuck You"*
*and Means It.* Ten, *Silence at Christmas,*
eleven, *The Shared Needle.* Twelve,
*Drunk at His Father's Funeral,*
and thirteen, I have to press it
against my ear its voice is so thin.
Thirteen is, *Mom, Do You Remember That Day*
*at the Park? It Was Your Birthday, I Think.*
*Do You Remember? How Small I Was,*
*How You Didn't Even Say "Thank You?"*

## GIRL INSIDE

My daughter is growing and everything is tender
so she cannot be touched. No more hugs. No more
playing with her hair as she reads a book.
She locks her door now. Stands in the mirror
and challenges the girl inside it to war, threatens
to cut down her nose, collects the flesh of her belly
in both hands and holds it up
like an auctioneer with a newborn pig.

When we moved to Brooklyn, she packed
her father's drawn out bones. They stretch
and knob and moan, delivering her good
angry face above all the other girls, eye-to-eye
with the shit-mouthed boys. My girl,
who wants to die all the time,
does not know—
breasts or no breasts, she will someday become
a worm in the heart of all she leaves behind.

## FINALLY, THE AUTHOR GETS PERSONAL

You should know: that morning,
in my bedroom, in that empty house,
I wanted you more than anything
an ordinary body could give.

The strange shock like starving arms
pulling, my stomach tight as a shark's—
I thought my body might be pulled inside-out
like a kitchen glove. Quiet, I bit
half-way through my tongue.

The papers chewed on me like the sweet
blood morsel I was—seventeen, honor roll.
I spoke to them with perfect posture. A good
student, told them I learned in books how to
tie the cord, used meat shears to cut it. Explained
the birthing positions I studied, how I kneeled
like a native. All the months of preparation.

None of that.

Lovely boy, you should know—
when your head appeared and your shoulders
cracked through my hips, I wasn't scared one bit.
Didn't need your father, who washed dishes, or
the girls who practiced suicide in my room.
I didn't need my boozy father, my wild brother.

Let me say: the Christmas Eve before you were born,
on my seventeenth birthday, when you hooked
your heel on the bottom rung of my ribs,
I knew I would not give you away.

And I realized what I was prepared to become.
Thief of my own body. A woman who could
pull a boy from herself, chew through his cord
with her love-sharp teeth.

# AFTERWORD

On October 22, 2021, at 12:50 a.m., I received the following text message from my brother Peter:

> *I've been too distraught to tell you that dad passed away at 2:42pm today.*

Pete Camacho Sr. was 67-years old when he died of COVID-19. Peter Jr. succumbed to the same virus seventeen days later. He was 44.

## FOR MY BROTHER AND FATHER, WHO DIED AND DIED

The news hammers me face-first
into the earth. Refusing to take root,
I cleave my way to the surface, reborn
No One's Daughter, No One's Sister.

*

For two nights, I'd shot up in bed at 7:44, sharp.
I felt it. Peter's final breath; my heart
thieved slowly from its velvet bag.

*

Is an absent mother permitted such instinct?
Did her newdead boy quake her gut in two?

*

After my men are fed to the kiln, I am all that remains.
Dab a spot of blood behind each ear and fuck like I'm dying.
My body a sideshow souvenir, the dead's wet amenity.
Their ashes clot the gaps between my reddest hours.

Once upon an awful time, they were the most holy
beings; their hoarded masculinity my earliest worship.
As I grew, girlhood—resistant to every act of
prohibition—softened me to chaos. Tits, hips
and a mouth without prayer:

betrayal
betrayal
betrayal

*

The reporter asks of our formative years:
*What were you like as children?*

/ We were never children /

Ask, instead, how heartless
the imagination can get.
How blue. A tortured pet
for the Sundays we
were bruised awake.
The pinched arm
of a beloved child
for the mother
who spat us out.

Ask why we sewed
the curtains shut,
never answer the phone

still.

*

My Peter slid down the bathroom wall, mouth
hung open, as if to eat those final strands of light,
while our mother, busy little siphoner,
crawled through his kitchen window.

*

Saddled by loss, I'm broken in.
Mourning gallops and gallops over me.

*

Dare I speak of inheritance?
What am I willing to pass down?
Why bother naming children
grandmother'd by schizophrenia?

I need who is mine to be only mine.

*

Once, I wrote how I threatened our father with a hammer.
Once, my brother asked if the story was true.
Once, both men forgot why the hitting died down.

Fragments are the shitty evidence of what is gone.
How can I become holy if I remain un-whole?

Darkness interrupts the light left in me.
I enter each day darkly. Carry
their terrible heads everywhere I go.
One skull fathers my right hand,
one skull brothers my left.

Cerberus of the 800 block,
I feast on loaves of honey cake,
help the dead stay dead.

*

There is nothing left to imagine. The truth is cold enough.

My father was dying,
his son watched, bedside,
and did nothing.

My brother, the quietest child.
My brother, the final hammer.

*

I still worry for Peter, alone in the morgue. Refrigerated, no clothes.
During the worst moments he survived as a boy, I was there.
I could not protect him but I was there,
a brutal chaperone. Small bodies, conjoined in terror.

It is wrong to grow older without him. He will always be behind.
Won't catch up, even after I am dead.

I cannot forgive this fact.

*

If grief must be the landscape, let delusion be the open road.

*

My dear brother

I choose to reside here, on this alternate planet, where I never answer the phone, ignore the coroner's unknown number for the rest of my days. Here, on the Planet of Unknowing, you are alive, no horrible news has taken you from me.

Here, I stroll through fields as your big sister, so plain and sacred. When I hug my children, they have an uncle who is breathing, full of noise.

On this Planet of Unknowing, I lie still in bed, 3,000 miles away. You are just an ordinary man eating a comforting meal, laughing at an old Eddie Murphy routine, your shoes next to the front door, pointing north.

Here, your body thrills with amnesia. In a few months, you won't remember how to flinch. There will be no broken lamp, no bloodmother's name to rot the vine. Here, the shrapnel of your earliest years slips from every wound. Lift your face to the loaded moon, my radiant heir of forgetting.

Peter, when I die, do not leave this planet to welcome me. Stay. Fall in love. Have too many children. Grow achingly old. Eat and eat and eat. Exist in our phoneless universe, where truth can never reach you.

button poetry

# CREDITS

**Assistant Editors**
Reese Brunette
Isabelle Keller
Melanie Koopmans
Alix Wolf

**Book Photography**
Emily Van Cook

**Cover and Interior Design**
Charley Eatchel
Amy Law

**Distribution**
SCB Distributors

**Ebook Production**
Siva Ram Maganti

**Publisher**
Sam Van Cook

**Publishing Operations Manager**
TaneshaNicole Kozler

**Publishing Operations Assistant**
Charley Eatchel

**Social Media and Marketing**
Nancy Nguyen
Eric Tu

## OTHER BOOKS BY BUTTON POETRY

If you enjoyed this book, please consider checking out some of our others, below. Readers like you allow us to keep broadcasting and publishing. Thank you!

Robert Wood Lynn, *How to Maintain Eye Contact*
Junious 'Jay' Ward, *Composition*
Usman Hameedi, *Staying Right Here*
Sean Patrick Mulroy, *Hated for the Gods*
Sierra DeMulder, *Ephemera*
Taylor Mali, *Poetry By Chance*
Matt Coonan, *Toy Gun*
Matt Mason, *Rock Stars*
Miya Coleman, *Cottonmouth*
Ty Chapman, *Tartarus*
Lara Coley, *ex traction*
DeShara Suggs-Joe, *If My Flowers Bloom*
Ollie Schminkey, *Where I Dry the Flowers*
Edythe Rodriguez, *We, the Spirits*
Topaz Winters, *Portrait of My Body as a Crime I'm Still Committing*
Zach Goldberg, *I'd Rather Be Destroyed*
Eric Sirota, *The Rent Eats First*
Neil Hilborn, *About Time*
Josh Tvrdy, *Smut Psalm*
Phil SaintDenisSanchez, *before & after our bodies*
Ebony Stewart, *WASH*
L.E. Bowman, *Shapeshifter*
Najya Williams, *on a date with disappointment*
Jalen Eutsey, *Bubble Gum Stadium*
Meg Ford, *Wild/Hurt*
Jared Singer, *Forgotten Necessities*
Daniel Elias Galicia, *Still Desert*
Chelsea Guevara, *Cipota*
Mickie Kennedy, *Glandscapes*
FreeQuency, *(On /Un-)Becoming*
Hailey Tran, *an everyday occurrence*
Kristina Percy, *Both True*
Gigi Bella, *without the frills*
Aly Acevedo, *My Dear Cult Leader*

Available at buttonpoetry.com/shop and more!

## BUTTON POETRY BEST SELLERS

Neil Hilborn, *Our Numbered Days*
Hanif Abdurraqib, *The Crown Ain't Worth Much*
Olivia Gatwood, *New American Best Friend*
Sabrina Benaim, *Depression & Other Magic Tricks*
Melissa Lozada-Oliva, *peluda*
Rudy Francisco, *Helium*
Rachel Wiley, *Nothing Is Okay*
Neil Hilborn, *The Future*
Phil Kaye, *Date & Time*
Andrea Gibson, *Lord of the Butterflies*
Blythe Baird, *If My Body Could Speak*
Rudy Francisco, *I'll Fly Away*
Andrea Gibson, *You Better Be Lightning*
Rudy Francisco, *Excuse Me As I Kiss The Sky*

# FORTHCOMING BOOKS BY BUTTON POETRY

Carson Wolfe, *Coin Laundry at Midnight*

Adrienne Novy, *good luck in the real world*

Available at buttonpoetry.com/shop and more!